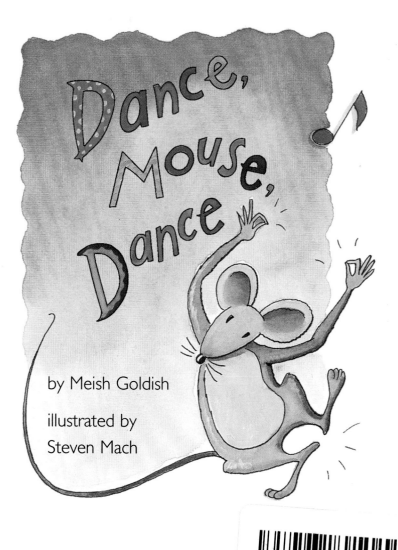

Dance, Mouse, Dance

by Meish Goldish

illustrated by
Steven Mach

Scott Foresman

Editorial Offices: Glenview, Illinois • New York, New York
Sales Offices: Reading, Massachusetts • Duluth, Georgia
Glenview, Illinois • Carrollton, Texas • Menlo Park, California

This cage is a house.
It is for Kim's mouse.

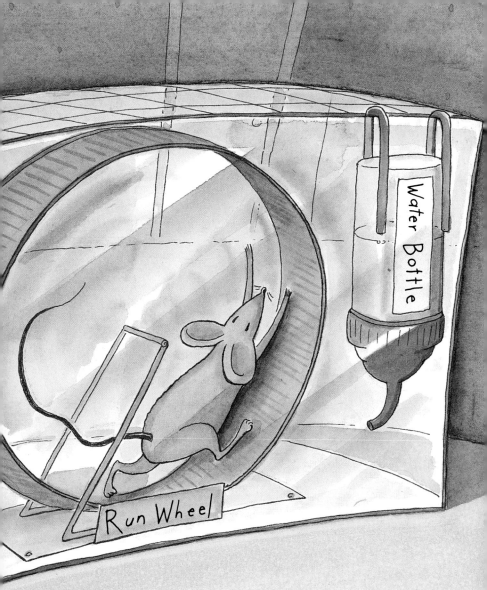

A bottle of water! A wheel to run!
Watch this mouse as she has fun.

See what this mouse can do!
She can dance like you.
Step in the cage and turn!
See what a mouse can learn!

Dance and dance all day.
Dance the hours away!
Step, go, turn!
See what a mouse can learn!

At night, Kim goes to sleep.
But her mouse goes out to creep.

It creeps out of the cage.
It would like to find a stage.

It dances near the house.
Look! There's another mouse!

Step, go, turn!
The mouse wants to learn.
Step, go, turn!
See what this mouse can learn!

In the dark, it's hard to see.
Look!
There's a bird up in the tree!

Step, go, turn!
The bird wants to learn.
Step, go, turn!
See what a bird can learn!

The mouse stays out all night.
The dark soon turns to light.

Where is Kim's mouse?
Stepping back into the house!

Look who is still asleep!
Look who is not making a peep.

Bottle

Run Wheel

Up comes the sun.
It is another day of fun!

Dance, mouse, dance!